THE IMPORTANCE OF ELSEWHERE

THE IMPORTANCE OF ELSEWHERE

Jerry Bradley

INK BRUSH PRESS

© 2009 Ink Brush Press

Temple, Texas

Library of Congress Cataloging-in-Publication Data

Bradley, Jerry, 1948 –
   Importance of Elsewhere / Jerry Bradley

   ISBN 978-0-9824405-0-6

   2009
   2009930690

Design by Minor Design

Acknowledgements

The author gratefully acknowledges the following publications in which versions of these poems appeared:

Ars Medica: "Washing the Cadavers"
Barkeater: The Adirondack Review: "… and Forty Nights"
Becoming: The Underground Journal: "Dissuade Shoes"
Burnside Review: "Life, Death, Time, Love, and Scenery"
CCTE Studies: "The Sex Researcher," "This Afternoon"
Chili Verde Review: "Simple Division," "Unmade Love"
Concho River Review: "Hark, Harold!" "Photographing the Cows,"
   "A Toast to Our Century"
Descant: "Bart's Night Out," "Lullaby," "Visit to a Church,"
   "Waiting for Snow at Night"
Different Worlds: "One for the Road," "Sunday Drive"
Eye: "Egg and Spoon"
The Family Therapy Networker: "At the Mental Health Clinic"
Iron Horse: "Buying a Vowel," "Cat as in Catastrophe," "I Never Think of My Father"
Kimera: "Calling in the Dark"
The Langdon Review of the Arts: "A Field Guide to Dreams," "Monet/Duet,"
   "Moon above Palo Duro," "Wherever the Spirit Travels"
The Legacy: "Burning Love"
The Listening Eye: "The Sorrow of Lobsters"
New England Review: "Dear Dad"
New Texas: "Earshot," "Rheum and Coca-Cola," "Self-Portrait with Spirits,"
   "Snowdeaf," "The Student Research Conference"
Paint Lick: "Rising Fish"
Poetry Magazine: "Eating Live Fish," "The Face of Vegetables," "What I Did Last Year,"
   "Witness for the Prosecution"
Porcupine: "Counting"
SCOL: Scholarship and Creativity On Line, A Journal of the Texas College English Association:
   "In My Place," "Procrastination," "The Sad Mistress"
The Sound of Poetry: "Meghan's New Shoes"
Southwestern American Literature: "If and Weather," "Last Flight Out"
Suddenly: "Vermeer in Vermont"
Taj Mahal Review: "Big Dogs Walk Late," "A Canyon View," "Drifter,"
   "The Voodoo Museum at Lent"
Texas Poetry Calendar 2010: "Flying with the Crows"
Texas Poetry Journal: "Antenna," "Disbelief"
Two Southwests: "Afterward," "Cleaving a Valentine," "A Single Sheep, One Cow,"
   "La Vida Nada"

for Barrie, golden alias of the sun

Contents

HOW THINGS WERE

I Never Think of My Father	1
Burning Love	2
Counting	3
Meghan's New Shoes	4
In My Place	5
At the Mental Health Clinic	6
Hark, Harold!	7
The Sad Mistress	8
Procrastination	9
The Face of Vegetables	10
Big Dogs Walk Late	11
Egg and Spoon	12
Drifter	13
Antenna	14
Dear Dad	15
A Toast to Our Century	16
The Difference between Real Life and TV	17

SOME FOR THE ROAD

If and Weather	21
What I Did Last Year	22
One for the Road	23
Eating Live Fish	24
Cat as in Catastrophe	25
Buying a Vowel	26
Sunday Drive	28
Vermeer in Vermont	29
Flying with the Crows	30
Wherever the Spirit Travels	31
The Voodoo Museum at Lent	32
Visit to a Church	34
Disbelief	35
Finding Your Way in the Dark	36
How To Talk So Kids Will Listen	37

WHAT THE DESERT SAW

Moon above Palo Duro	41
Last Flight Out	42
Vacation	43
Photographing the Cows	44
Life, Death, Time, Love, and Scenery	45
Waiting for Snow at Night	46
Dissuade Shoes	47
This Afternoon	48
Witness for the Prosecution	49
Afterward	50
A Canyon View	51
Earshot	52
Snowdeaf	53
Cleaving a Valentine	54
Rising Fish	55
La Vida Nada	56
Lullaby	57
Self-Portrait with Spirits	58
Diving into Love	60
The World's Worst Roadside Attraction	61

THE HIBISCUS DATELINE

A Field Guide to Dreams	65
Bart's Night Out	66
The Sex Researcher	67
Monet/Duet	68
Calling in the Dark	69
The Sorrow of Lobsters	70
Simple Division	71
... and Forty Nights	72
Rheum and Coca-Cola	73
Washing the Cadavers	74
The Student Research Conference	76
How To Make Love to the Same Woman Forever	77

how things were

I Never Think of My Father

I never think of my father as young
though the photos prove otherwise:
here posed in a sleeveless undershirt
and khakis, a teenager already three years deep
in the Army but no kid, just another
Kentucky hardballer smoking his way
down the road to Depression and World War.

In another he kneels in front of several Chevrolets,
smirking as if he'd spent the whole evening
chasing moonshine with his loony pals
and trying to embrace the night's fat ass.

I never think of my father as old either.
Dead at sixty-two, he was smileless
long before the hospital, durably stern
and disapproving as if he suspected everyone
had been pissing off the porch.

*I want to hear nothing but silence,
and plenty of it,* he scolded all my youth.
He has likely had his fill of it now.

I think of my father forever somewhere
in the middle of middle age, burning
between flame and frost like Dantean hell,
his heart the equator of a world
he could not hold together or a polar ice cap,
an imaginary line, geographically absent
and remembered, whenever I think of him,
only in a poem, frowning. Sometimes
not even the memory of happiness will do.

Burning Love

In the fifth grade while the rest of us
craved baseball and candy,
Glenn fell in love. During recess
he kissed a girl behind the trees;
she had begun to grow breasts,
though he was too young to do much about that
or them. He was enchanted instead by her name
and wrote *Sue* again and again
on book covers; he daydreamed about marriage
in history and math. He even scratched
her name on a mesquite's skin with a fork
he swiped from his lunchroom tray.
Then in what passed for passion in those days,
he fashioned the heads of kitchen matches
into a tattoo on his wrist.

She gave off more heat than light.
Unimpressed by the blisters that
spelled her irrevocably into a scar,
she kissed another boy on the school bus home.
Glenn cried when he heard. He tried not to,
but he did. First heartbreak is always sad;
still he sensed how much worse
it might have been. Then he called himself lucky,
so lucky he hadn't fallen for Elizabeth.

Counting

Sheep are for farmers. I awake from waves,
the ebbing of tidal pools, to count my way

out of youth and drift untethered in the surf
in and out, mostly out, the length of an ocean,

nearly drowning in apnea,
lacking air and, always a bad swimmer,

wresting from the kelp any breath
that might not strangle as certainly as matted fleece.

Awash in a methane sea of miniature
seahorses and bergs grinding

with all that rafted ice, blue and green
like lozenges in a latrine,

I flail, a sodbuster, all arms,
fighting rain and the eddying wind,

the hammer of the humpback whale,
my old buoyant heart steadily

losing against the current.
Though no longer young,

I am not completely washed up:
I still risk dreaming you into bed

where, knees to stomach, you round
like a conch in my embrace.

Moses had it easy. Breaking the sea
was easier than dividing us now,

counting sheep harder than counting waves
when time is always on the ocean's side.

Meghan's New Shoes
— For Keith Carter

when smoke relaxes
it comes back
tired of leaving the world
its top opens
like present string
and falls away

when light wakens
it falls all at once
grown old in the flash
of its first moment

on my birthday
I rose like smoke
aching to be grown
but when the light
of these Mexican sparklers folded
I fell back like gravity
into the world
and into these new shoes

In My Place

In no rush for first coffee, she says she slept
on it and decided I had been wrong all along,
then told me just how much: 360 degrees.
It was just her way of speaking, like saying,
if the round world were to end, she'd hate for me
to miss it — sweet in its own way. Still
she couldn't resist bringing me up on charges.
Short of that, nagging was always a promise kept.

Unlike the world, what I was wrong about passed,
but how wrong I was did not. I expected to find myself
on the opposite side of the earth yelling *is so!* across
some ocean's great abyss. Instead from home latitude
a whisper did it, an intimacy, just two people sharing
a single thing — even though one of us is clearly wrong.

At the Mental Health Clinic

rows over a woman shapes curses
into a bark, her belongings
in bags around her feet
another sobs over a dead cat
I sit with the pyromaniac teen
too old to be in love again
and hurting like the rest

we have been asked to speak
about our dreams
to squeeze the bruise
of childhood into words

to hear each other say
(as we always do)
that the cure cringes within
hiding like our hardened hearts

but there may not be room enough
for all of us here
for everyone's pain

irremediable and afraid
we sit like dead mice
on the doorstep now

without visible scars
but helpless still
having gone too far beyond ourselves
and into someone else's yard

Hark, Harold!

The season of reindeer and carols,
Of glazed slush that thaws, then gathers against the curb.
The crosstown malls are jammed, but here
Below an idling downtown building
I peer alone through a security grate
At a drugstore version of Christmas —
St. Nick riding a new shaver
Jollily down a slope of cotton toward
Depilatories and shampoos and throw-away cameras
Meant to catch that special face beneath the tree,
Its beatific Chinese grin fixed long
beyond the contraption that flashed it.
Tags dangle from every notion and cologne,
Each product a potential present. I read
The names and think of absent friends,
The unexpected gifts that fell upon us
Once like love. I tell my dead mother
I'll be home this year for sure and pass
Unnoticed from this sad display to another
On a street where now not even Santa knows my name.

The Sad Mistress

tasting of mercurachrome, her kiss
maneuvers across flesh and cheerless muscle
just so much day labor
migrating toward nightfall

like the alewife who spilled the sugar
she tracks anguish into every room
in the kitchen one bottle holds thyme,
another her onion tears
she writes letters to herself
on the bathroom mirror

even when I hold her melting
marshmallow breasts
she thinks about crying

her heart is a wound
she says that will not heal

she cannot touch where it hurts
because she lives on the wrong side
of the mattress, a tag warning
do not remove under penalty of law

Procrastination

My mother told me I'd never amount to much,
my lazing grown enormous in her eyes. She couldn't
see what I was practicing to become: a yogi
concentrating his power and strength,
an elephant in reserve eating peanuts and chips,
downing whatever was nearby — preferably salted —
and ghazaling cold beverages to wash it all down.
And when I was full, my sutra sang about the cessation
of hunger, not my mother's nearly tripping on the rake
I had abandoned by the door. And nighttime, gazing
at the stars — mostly the TV kind — I felt the hold
of the universe, something astral, the warm sun
reflecting the motion of our cooling planets.

My mother was never one to disambiguate the world.
While I meant through indolence, study, and self-reflection
to overcome ignorance and conceit, every obstruction,
she knew the lethargy in my bones. "Get up, fool," she'd say.
But even Beowulf caught hell for not taking out the trash.
"I'll be someone someday, Mama," I said, renouncing my fate.
"I will. You'll see. Just you wait. Just you wait."

The Face of Vegetables

I have been brave in the face of vegetables,
known the rancor of crucifers and kale,
the cold shoulders of cauliflower,
have witnessed the steamy jealousy of carrots
and the derisive blanch of garden squash,
the calumny of beets and their sugary bite,
the acrid taste of turnips bleeding in my mouth.
I have seen broccoli, onions bunching and bulbing,
the wince of rhubarb in summer's heat.

She said love would not wither, a green thing
to bloom and grow, but, when she began to leaf,
I weakened like a collard indoors
and wept; though I wilted in my tears,
I burned like a dumbcane in drought.

Big Dogs Walk Late

"The moon is the only traveler without a passport" — Ramon Gomez de la Serna

It is dangerous to pursue more love than there is.
You can try to wash its alphabet from your mouth,
but when you recall the house where you were born,
you speak of a boy with a bucket and an old straw hat
who wishes the water would hold still on its way
from the well. Your granddad waves from atop
a wagon of hay, his tractor long-settled in the scrapyard
by the barn. The harnessed mules sense a rareness
in the air. Enchantingly, there are no pigs;
a few cows are arranged in the usual manner.

You filled your pockets with warm rocks to stay
the west wind's drift but staggered like a bumpkin
in a country reel or wild timothy swept up
by a horsetail's swirl. Grandmother's briary flowers
freckled your flesh and your rollicking ragweed heart.
At night the costive sky distended with stars;
the tv spoke of alien intruders. It was a time
when the biggest dogs walked late.

The first morning you set out from home
you felt its tremor in your fingers.
The sun rose on the wrong side of the house;
upstairs someone made ready the funeral bench.
You wrote letters, began to answer yourself,
but now all you can do is listen to the anguish
as it tries to howl away the past.

You caught its terror, and you have it in you now.
The nursing home is full of people just like you;
their families gather like buzzards on an ass's rump.
You try to remember the vows you made
and just when it was you signed on to receive
the certified message of sorrow. Look at the sky
and babble. See how the moon distracts.
Spell it, say the word. Empty means just what it says.

Egg and Spoon

Something so fine-spun as an egg
is suspicious cargo; it perplexes,
even at rest

like the cup-curdling veil of milk
in an advertisement
for a Chinese teahouse on Main.
Everything commercial clouds the motif
light makes, but on the tabletop
the spoon's response is stirring;

inside the pin-pricked shell
hazy baby teeth grow hardboiled,
and something as insensate as the moon

and notional as the scars of lobsters
warms and rounds with desire.
There is no protecting the old angels;

whatever fell on them weighs
them down like childhood now,
but what they carry in their cuspids

unnerves. Milky and ovoid, they are like
a hotel of sleeping children readying
to wake and mouth coddled prayers.

Drifter

The thaw drips off the melting roof and plops
within earshot of the door. *Don't let it in.*
It is a woman with white hair nursing an old dispute.

The ground is a hem of thin linen
that spreads toward the silos and scrub
to sully the barnyard's dress.

The mirroring ice complains
like a bad joint. *Call the boys
before I am too old, too old.*

A coughing accordion
in the shutters, the wind
plays its old refrain.

But this warm bed holds more
than a beggar's wintry rants.
Though the stars close in the cold,

tonight we can kiss them closer.
See how the sky shakes
the snow out of her hair.

Antenna

The sleepless forgo music,
    have no need of its backward glance
and stuttering refrains.

What they want is all-night chat,
    tales of alien abduction,
the word on crop circles,

sightings from Area 51,
    radar reports above Gulf Breeze
and Tenochtitlan,

government secrets in eyes-only
    binders. What I thought
was a nighthawk

lacked signature, though it may
    have been something more.
The Weekly World News

says it saw what I caught
    briefly in my brights
before I swerved.

Most folks dream archaisms:
    the stainless coaches of the '50s
still move along rails for them

like the sleepy signals from still space
    or the sounds from a radio
so distant that

it remembers only itself
    before leaving us behind
intent and listening

in the ever-widening night.

Dear Dad

Dear Dad
    Life is hard. Clouds bonnet my school
in a nightmare. Though invisible at
night they are still there lurking
when I close my eyes. I have seen
Mom again in my dreams. This one
begins in a field where we hide in
the brush waiting. She is a bird.
When she comes over, we open up on
her. The first shell hits her square,
and she falls, quick and painful in
her airy dismount. A shower of feathers
flashes in the safety of my stare.
The something I see when I blink is
the something I see when I don't.
Mornings are spent at the lake. They
have run out of cinnamon rolls for
breakfast, so we all must fish.
Bluegills and coffee before noon,
rainbows after. The warden stops
a boy wearing my cap, holding my
reel. What's the matter, kid? Can't
you read the sign? Today the dean
has canceled classes while they
search the blind for more bodies.
The skies call for rain, and there
are no more rolls. My roommate waits
in ambush, gunning for my grades. If
the fish don't bite, I will have to fly
soon, free of memory like Mom prematurely
blown from the public trust. Money is low.
Write soon.
                        Your Son

A Toast to Our Century

Tomorrow when the children find this snow
and wake happily to a sky that leans
toward blue, cloudless but friendly and full of peace,
they will not think of tonight's drowsy storm.
Sleeping in the disobedient warm,
they are fixed in a new year that they know
will give all their fears and nightmares release.

The grown yearn to slumber without deep dreams —
older, wise at last, sad, confused, and slow,
they fall up into the old century
like contrary flakes gone wrong in the snow.
And weary from twelve hundred months of pain,
they rise like bubbles in this toast's champagne
before a last salute and all darkness comes down.

The Difference Between Real Life and TV

I have a tv

some for the road

If and Weather

Both night and day are black and filled with climatic noise,
The isobar a dim clue on heartbreak's stormy map;
A man tires of toys, may kiss his wife into the moon
While stars seen solely in darkness fall into his lap.

But sometimes out of pain only adversity comes.
Without notice its unrepentant forecast unfurls,
And west becomes east as it passes through our center,
Its flesh like the rounded circumference of a girl

Or a squall named for a woman whose cyclonic love
Is a watercolor, a framed barometric print.
Your fragrant swirl bails out the world every time it floods.
Moment after moment like the first moment is meant
For the dark. I sleep in your wake, feeling sorry for
Everyone who isn't me and the someone who is.

What I Did Last Year

Below the old psychiatric hospital
and spring mansions in bloom
the river rolls like an enormous shudder
between two Midwestern states
separating towns named upon a time
for presidents and poets

Near the Civil War encampments
littered with sheep droppings
and Greek revival homes
it barges through sulking summer
toward bigger cities
where diluent water birds
disgorge their contaminated prey
past fields stretching with warm grass
and dockland children
and dry-footed men talking to worms

    away from the nomad students
    and their famous fountain
    whose water falls upon itself
    as gently as petals on a plinth

On Old Main anonymous beds
of strangers lull near breakfast
like love in a Victorian diary
always expecting something more

For them the Ohio is just a bookmark
a black nightdress, an enormous taxi
whose speeding engine conceals
that everything is farther away
than it once was

And now out of reach
they are amazed
that it was ever within it

One for the Road

When the copter left and we were alone,
glacial ice splitting under our feet
and rinsing, rushing into the cavern's green glaze,
I thought of margaritas, the beach,
Puerto Vallarta's endless surf.
In moonboots and slicker I expected
a distant constellation, a landscape
pocked and lunar, ravaged, not the slush
of tequila in an icy lagoon.
                    But home
is so strange; tired of it, we leave
only to find ourselves reflected in chips
and cubes at every destination
and in return bringing part of what
was already us back to itself.
So when the pilot reappeared, lowering
with a friendly wave, we boarded
blooming with excitement and tipsy
from the cold while the swizzle of the rotor
lifted us once more and stirred our memory
like a strong drink.

Eating Live Fish

beyond the transom the neighbor
in 6-B dines with foreigners
in a room alive with flies

they buzz like
the Sao Paolo slums

the apartment is crowded
probably full of criminals
or worse

lawbreaking outlanders
who have given the law the slip

they understand this country
came to it on hard decks
looking for money

and hoping to grow old
but they are full of dry prayers

the one with the scar
nods knowingly
wears an artificial flower

you think you've seen him before
you know his kind

but the fan's slow blades remind
that there is a world
you don't recognize

language that pierces
and gabbles like barnyard fowl

you wonder what goes on
beyond their door
wonder if you turned the knob
you'd find them eating live fish

Cat as in Catastrophe

Never learning from experience
I shoot west through chopped fields
wondering how Texas ever got so flat.
To the east the generic haircuts and cafeterias
of Dallas, Abilene, and Lubbock fire and reload;
homes in between like rearview lanterns go black.

Farther out the sky broods like a glancing god:
the sullen clouds hiss wherever its light is spilled,
paper chickens swirl like fate, and
shuck lizards, wilder than a Sunday prayer
for money, race roadward to be killed.

Even the wheels tire of it all. In New Mexico
far from any station or track
rail cars hold seed, saddles, and tack;
satellite dishes squat next to adobes,
their sandstruck foundations shifty and eroded.
Along the highway disabled pickups curse and crawl,
threaten to finish us off. Farther west
the atomic bomb first exploded

Buying a Vowel

Armchairs and crosswords at twenty thousand,
you try to ignore the trip, the report
of lightning outside, a city with ghastly cuisine ahead,
the side windows full of bad clouds
through which you would fall should the pilot doze
or his great machine fail. You ponder
a four-letter word for French Sudan
and look forward at comb marks, seat backs, and scalps
as the steward's mouth spills messages
    into the uncaring yawn.

The microphone is broken today, he says,
but everything else is all right.
There will be drinks and safety —
plenty of safety — and plastic dropping into our laps
to save our panicky brains should such measures
become necessary. He locks a shortened belt
which he afterward releases with a smile and an easy thumb,
all the while saying something we can't quite make out.
His voice scatters among the rows, then dies.
    It is like trying to lipread a muppet.

What is beneath you seems far but is close enough — worksites
and homes, the town in which you were reared,
wrecked angles of patched farms on its edge,
the sprawling interstates you would use
to flee earthly disaster. But today you can afford peril;
you pay for the privilege of strangers. You dine
on the void as if it were a small edible flatfish
from a nameless Pacific atoll, a meal
    you chew but refuse to swallow.

If it were night, you might trick yourself
that the darkness comforts and the beacon consoles.
But there would be stars, always stars,
vaster than anything below and farther away than help.
And when the sky dreams, no words come.

Your questions drop like sunken treasure;
all the squares stare back as you fumble
in your seat like a crumbling pilaster in a foreign plaza.
This flight, you fear, like all blanks is numbered.
Your mouth draws to an **O**, and you wonder
    if forty-eight is really headed down.

Sunday Drive

traveling over a land teeming with color
we follow the map's direction

toward backroads and bayous
and into the flowering confection

of thickets that lure us with thorns
every sidetrack heavy with the pledge

of something we should not miss
and every flower and tree

named, every last one
sweeter than a calorie on our tongues

as we push further still
into our dessert

reading the guide, alert
for the waterfall, the mill

the scenic overlook
over the ridge

where a disused barn,
idle cows and a covered bridge

herald the stopping point
and our unnamed X

a tree bulging with the prospect
of our picnicking in its shade

and a nap of chocolate and outdoor sex
there within close reach

where afterward like sufficient cows
we drowse into waves

and elaborate the lazy lake
like petals dreaming a peach

Vermeer in Vermont

Light drenched, the Taconic's blues
are like babies in incubators,
the sun a golden rump,
and the Green Mountain granite
just so much quarry flesh
fallen from a backbone
into leaves the color of marbled meat.

The world would seem bigger
if one of your forty
had been painted here,
the hermit thrush happy
as pigment or soft cloth,
and the clover red as blood
or your girl's famous hat.

Narrow as a parenthesis,
Vermont would be a jar of paint,
a window of earthlight,
but your brush would not touch
its river or the dark oars
stroking toward shore.

Wise antediluvian,
you foresaw flood and wide water
and drew the colors around you
until they took the shape of land
and aboard your canvas ark
blushed like bright sin,
safe and drawn to the shelter
of your curving hand.

Flying with the Crows

That first night we roosted to dreams of grain,
And the blackest dropped down his head where we
Huddled as one. It was too cold for rain.

My feathers shivered when they fell, dark coal
Mined from the hole of the year, and hunger
Rotated like a cash crop in my soul.

Ah, but the plums, fixed fast in their sweetness
By the chill! And the thicket where they hung
Not a keen moment's flapping to the west.

Skins, pulp — a supermarket for the beak,
The savory allure of dull hides
Inviting us to fold dun winter's speech.

Turn cows on the corn — doughy, sad, and slow ...
My appetite rumbles like a taut drum,
My caws brighter than the snare of snow.

Wherever the Spirit Travels

wherever the spirit travels when it is done
the body stays in place

the pastor thinks he's a weatherman
and promises everything will be sunny

so it doesn't surprise that churches are for the dead
I'll probably be in heaven before another church

even if you change the names on the graves
I'll still be able to point where my people are
all still lying on their backs like a roach

I hear that Christ marries every priest and nun
but I'm looking for a different arrangement — a God with benefits
not one always threatening to shape his fingers into a gun

the man with his finger on the trigger should be an atheist's son

The Voodoo Museum at Lent

Beneath the alligator head and broom
the girl in the humid gift shop beckons.
"Start at the wishing stump," she says.
"Shake the rain stick if you want,
but leave the rest alone. Come back
to me when you've done it all."

I pay for her blessing and make a cemetery wish,
then pass among the talismans and oils,
skulls, shaman books and fool's hair,
powders, charms, and incense,
the translucent blowfish *ju-ju* with a startled face.

In the altar room the Voodoo Popess
Marie Laveau poses above candles;
blue portraits of lesser queens
protect a spirit box in a doll case.

I think of the rum West African slaves
offered their dead, the protection saints
promised for cigars and good money,
and how they must have resisted
the divination of Christ until
like my North Atlantic ancestors
intercession must have seemed
odder than an island of hurricanes,
blowzy fruit, and blackened palms.

All gods wear masks in wet climates,
and anyone's pricked finger may write
a *ve-ve* or gospel, but Marie's face
is as serene as a martyr's, like dryness
before the coming storm.

So when I light the votive, I think first
of myself, resisting the urge to surrender
and step back into the sultry store.
When I do, the girl again smiles,
offers an amulet for safe travel.

I bow as she places it around my neck
and makes a sign on my forehead with her thumb,
but it is an ashen show of faith.
What she wipes away might be sweat
or, I suspect, something even wetter.

Visit to a Church

Deaf as a stone, quartz is a kind of saint,
lost light chipped by air. What was it you said
about limestone, onyx, agate, and flint
and how the water drips its sad complaint
before it gathers like wine into bread?

Which gods are honest and which ones false,
and whose words are those that make us quake and lose
our vestments in quarries and chapel halls,
along the waterway of canyon walls,
the hard path up? What if we cannot choose?

Do you know what is sun and what is stone?
If you dream yourself between rock and ray,
the slightest facet seems great chalcedony;
your prayers at first adamantine, then gone,
a wafer tumbling toward a wayward sea

Disbelief

You've seen the signs there on every corner
warning of danger in the unseen breeze,
the falling rock that snaps your attention,
the oddest colors that no longer shock,
bold, bright, solid as all geometry,
but sensible too, meant to confer shape
to life, to confirm the right road, our way
of behaving, to square adversity
and keep us from slaloming through the curves
at unsafe speed. Even cloudy cafes
and flypocked roadside tables charm,
as do historic sites, menus, and markers.
For all our stalling and despite the assuring stripes
they stand to remind that most roads
remain dark. The physics of our safety
is always understood too late. Our fears
circle in traffic until they collide
like two strangers at an intersection,
uninsured and witless as bystanders,
having recklessly missed Beware of Dog
until disbelieving at last they see the teeth.

Finding Your Way in the Dark

Like the devil, you know
how to leave the road
and cross the thawing ditch,
the fence, the long field home.

    You fear the weight of stars,
but like them you want to burn,
set your kettles rattling and steaming,
and boil your beer-soured roots to broth.

    But the candescent god between your fingers
fears the dark, hurries it to flame.
When you strike, something inside you
shudders like a moth, and something matchless
dares you to call it by its name.

How To Talk So Kids Will Listen

speak loudly
speak very, very loudly

what the desert saw

Moon above Palo Duro

A hammered medallion,
the moon hangs above a place
the wind and water want back.

Night here sings of the forge,
and sounds of the anvil echo
along the canyon walls —

it plays like a stone fiddle
in a month of short days.

Just another big bang theory,
a lesson in circumference.
And see the stars, how they splinter

like sparks from the hearth?
It is where God struck his tarnished coin
before he beat the daylights out of the land.

Last Flight Out

Across this distance beer trucks disappear
and nomadic streams weave their lonely routes:
orchards and struggling farms, lava beds
that glisten in the heat.

                      It must have been hard
then, less hospitable, so many spear
points and arrows buried beneath. Thousands,
the desert still turns them with its feet.

                            But fired at what?
Game scarce and their aim so obviously bad,
what could they have hoped to hit?

                            Or was it
loneliness the vast gulf they shot
across, wider than any river or fence,
and some heart on the other side
waiting to be struck? In each quiver
something sought its mark and leapt,
and in discharge left nothing in the air,
not even cupid's fingerprints

Vacation

The guidebook said there were things not to miss
if I had the time — monuments, parks, dams,
the striking view from the aerial tram,
sun, clouds, and blunt peaks nearby below which
golf, the famous UFO landing site
await, places everybody should go.
And don't forget the friendly casino
whose neon aces beckon in the night.

What the desert saw was this: a trail
cold as one of the mountain's many stones,
ghost towns, a bullet from a narrow gauge
shell speeding as if along a greased rail,
graveyards with flush toilets at the trailhead
teeming with the silent, historic dead.

Photographing the Cows

In this landscape they have meteors for eyes,
not blazing but ones that have hit earth and cooled.
Heads up like heavy lanterns, they stand and gaze
at you, improvising thought, tails churning flies.
One skull seems not enough. This outcrop they graze
is as blank as frostscrawl or loaves of bread.
All doubt fades before hooves and horn, is not fooled
by the sounds of wind, wind on wheat, on grasses.

They smile, but they do not need your curving lens;
there is nowhere for them to go, won't say cheese.
They browse but are not led, ignore what passes,
are the negative your shot snaps. And their prints
pucker and pleat, gather, wander where they please,
trail to water, the sky they fell from like lead.

Life, Death, Time, Love and Scenery

Summer knows more than one trick. Leaning
against a rock beneath an unnatural sky,
you spread your blanket before you in picnic,
eat berries and cream, and watch water fall
from parchment cliffs onto the otter camps below.
You feel the shudder of exhausted wind
(which is nothing itself) unravel in the hayfields
where the dog star waits for night, winking unseen
    like a battery gone bad overhead.

When you read about places like this, you recall
the blonde who got sick in your truck,
its old gearbox groaning and bracing itself
against boulders in the washed-out road. Strapped
in her seat belt, she rinsed her mouth, eyes closed,
with the last swallow in the pint. You forgave
the frostbite in her dizzying kiss and thought
    this is how things are just before they come apart.

But because life is a place that recurs over time,
you remember her too in the smell of hot metal
and burning oil, in the once upon a time
when her lips were the open cylinder of a gun,
and when you wash yourself in the stream, just where
it narrows into a pool like your constricting heart,
you hear the lies she spoke all August,
aloud again as the dragonflies skim and dunk,
    and you try to cleanse yourself in the blood of want.

Waiting for Snow at Night

radiant in the moon
the patient stars
swing toward morning

the night seems as tame
as the bitten frost

bundled together and noiseless
beneath candles, electricity gone

we feel the drafts rattle
our teeth and bones

and wonder how everything
got so calm

the world seems to long
for such snowfall light

but maybe it's just
its desire for nothing

a need to find a word
great enough to hold

all its darkness
and all our cold

Dissuade Shoes

you don't know some places hurt
until you touch them

walking the land in new boots
you come to the catchment where cows
if you had any could drink

there would be grass and reeds
if there were water
and a place for nests

it is the same walk of long ago
before something stirred

before you came back
to this empty basin
to loiter, to wait
to imagine yourself a snake

you wish you had a knife
just in case
in case something
in the reeds there below your heart
might move, might strike
your boot, the top, the last

This Afternoon

the clouds roll
take shape and dissolve
tumble like gymnasts in the heat

if you listen you can hear corn
and see chilies swelling
rising to become sweet

there may be rain
there may be none
the world decides how it will move

it changes
to be beautiful
wanting ever to be lovelier than you

Witness for the Prosecution
—for Richard Bodner

Eyes fixing in the dark,
we saw the Japanese comet
in the north sky
moving from Dragon Mountain
across your land
toward the Mother Tree,
the overturned dipper
spilling milk onto its tail.

We couldn't believe how easy
it was to see the argument of night
unthread in the canopy overhead.
Ten thousand years ago
our species saw it first
before it came to us again
like an ex-wife with a new name.
We joked about catching it
the next time around,
wondering in whose eyes
we might be dilating then.

Back in the grapevine trailer
freezing in my blanket and shoes,
I thought of you and Virginia
wedded to each other and the world
and how that comet might have felt
heading from this place to one
somewhere else. I thought about
what I knew of loneliness,
and my lungs ached within my chest,
although it might have been my heart.

Afterward

The dandelions bow
to the whirring blade
as I walk the mower

across the lawn
trying to beat
the approaching storm.

It is not fall
but soon will be —
in an hour perhaps.

So the lizard
seeks his shelter
under the chipped pot,

and frogs abandon
their dream of meeting
their lovers by the river.

Summer has been so hot
we all have had tropical thoughts:
chocolate-covered mangoes,

naked silhouettes in the shade,
crickets enjoying
their picnic in bed.

When the cold comes
and the distant mountains
whisper to the wind,

the dim anarchy of change
will already be upon us, and
we will defect like the leaves

until change too passes
and afterward
a small radio announces rain.

A Canyon View

from here light
spreads like sorrow

it is a river of shadows

the sea is so close
we will not need a boat

but once we step
from this place
there will be
no retrieval or rescue

there will be only land
with dark water above
dark water and wetness
wetness all around

Earshot

The contrail eddies and bends its back,
then opens its fist and spiders
into a noiseless dot. The missile
we never saw thrusts toward Utah,
its dummy warhead punching holes
in blue September's clouds. Tracing its climb
with a finger, we watch the sky open,
then clot close behind.
                        When we hiked
the canyon wash that day, your dog spooked
rabbits, dozens, from their pm shade. Then the rain
erased her tracks and ours.
                        What we want,
we say, is a warning shot, thunder beating light
down the arroyo in time for us to hear what comes.
But what hides best is sound — the crack of the bullet
is never first to reach the heart. Like the picture tube
dissolving in the quicksand of itself, it goes deaf
before blind.
                        Dumb instrument, the tongue's
too subtle a thing; it means to report
what someone needs to hear but always arrives late,
just as something lovely has gone out of sight,
leaving it to stammer in the rinsing rain,
you were the most wonderful person in the world.

Snowdeaf

Separated from the drove, the angus calf
cries all night, his mother dead he fears,
fallen in the snow somewhere

shy of the warm lot and the hay-filled barn.
She does not answer his weakening call.
Even the young know the dead cannot return,

but still he bawls and bawls for the lost herd,
the other newborns, and the cozy udder,
afraid of the dark and its jagtooth eyes

harbored in the thicket of warm mesquites.
Stepping away from the drifting fence,
he measures a farm he has barely known,

sways as the wind whips the hardening flakes,
freezes the slobber to his chin,
his thin eyes frosting. The crystals click

like the second hand on a watch. This is a farm
without cemeteries, a place where the dead vanish.
Cattle trucks carry survivors to stockyards and slaughterhouses,

and cow families split like thin ice, their plaintive
protests ignored by the idling motor,
the old bull roaring, the herd dog's bark.

Cleaving a Valentine

This is no day for distance. Your reward
for six years of sick separation
is these chocolates I send and a card

recalling how much the far-off heart can bear.
Tell me, what is love but what we've conferred
upon ourselves to make our drab lives dear?

And why must these scarlet letters suggest disease?
We telephone passion when we know
valentines are better carved upon trees

(though in West Texas only those planted,
staked, watered by hand, and plotted will grow).
You think I have taken love for granted,

though I contend I have loved you enough
for anyone's life but mine. There's in me,
I say, a pit, a seed of something rough,

too wide and vast to hear its own sad bark.
It grows slow like love but is more enduring
and sturdier than any time-cleft heart.

Rising Fish

the water breaks like a smile
recrudescent as champagne
but opaque
and scattering the trees
in this tranquil place

one finds in such immensity
every sort of motion and dumb eyes
marks that disguise a nation

and the silver chevron of a trout
drops back like a sling
into the lake

arcing in celebration
like a deserter
from a doused division

a private whose lingual journey
moves inward along
the bottle's sticky rim
threatens to pop the cork
and make the whole pool grin

La Vida Nada

my dreams burn like green chili
but still play hard to get
my ambition barely acknowledges
its own presence in the mirror

my flirtation with success
is never taken seriously
let's just be friends
she repeats whenever I call

pennies fall through my pockets
as if they were jack-o-lantern's eyes
paper money won't keep out the cold

my father's belt that wore me out
when I came home with C's
barely keeps me tied to my own ass

my horoscope predicts legions of lost loves
holds an aberrated future
hostage on its parchment

my semi-career (quasi-civilian)
sits in fatigues ready to blow me away
with no remorse for its terror

disease has already set foot
on the basement stair
flies gather around the hole
in my open fantasy

when anyone asks how I died
just say I strangled on my potential

Lullaby

The autumn has been so fine
the bears will not sleep.
Behind the house
lambs have learned their song
and berries spread thick syrup,
crimson, ruby-maroon, and deep.
The garden is as sodden
as a savory pie.

All summer spring has been
running down, the dipper
spilling its honey
across the sky. The night
fills its jar with starry fruit.

But it is a world of change,
and time obliges. Turning
like a girl on a stair,
it counts its steps like sheep
huddling under a longitude of stars;
then they hurdle one another
across the sky
as she twines her hair
and counts her way to sleep.

Self-Portrait with Spirits

The séance is for believers only,
the house haunted by a distraught rancher
who killed, we are told, his wife and himself
more than ninety years ago. His spirit
will not rest. It moans. It slams heavy doors
and moves things. It paces the upper floors.

Like it I too empty glasses; shiraz
warms in my palms as I mull the notion
of a water-swilling ghost. The good ones,
our hostess claims, dwell solely in the dark,
and, if this spot is where essences are drawn,
we may have to stay awake until dawn.

No madam, she spreads a bedsheet
across the table and lights three candles,
as if it were 1968: cinnamon, she says,
for warmth and vigor; for meditation
and peace, frankincense;
the sandalwood smells like Phoenix

where in Molly's bed we lay doped out
one spring break. But the explanation
is too New Age: all things divisible
by three are holy. But why,
why are Dead People drawn to primes?
Because they too are superstitious, she reminds.

So tonight I have questions and slow time.
And there may be answers — we'll have to see,
but even the friendly spirits won't stay
if we are not polite. Trust the palanche,
the ouija, see what the video screen
reveals, what we may not have heard or seen.

But why are DP's so angry?
And what's the objection to being numb,
the source of their unease? How frustrating
to be so incensed and still so — well — dead,
gone to the beyond with still much to prove.
What is in this glass? Who makes it move?

Diving into Love

you stand on the rail
dreaming what will happen
when you bottom in the shallows
strangling on your necklace of stars

how the drop will crack you
like adobe where the HazMat team
waits on the rocks
to gather your remains

you fear what your heart has to say
what will happen if you fall
back into yourself

what will happen
if you don't

and licking the salt from your palms
you cross your fingers
like you do at bingo
and plunge

hoping to be lucky
if only for tonight
when you open the motel door

but already knowing
how the tequila bites
just like a South Valley girl

The World's Worst Roadside Attraction

Carl's bad caverns

the hibiscus dateline

A Field Guide to Dreams

a man owes something to his dreams

waking in the strange night or shivering in a stream,
he is blind beyond the curve where the hyacinth gathers

and the river becomes a boring stretch of road
its curve is the like the curve of her leg

and when in sleep you swim
the long shadow upstream to her

and away from the sneer of fish
you become something orchestral

the water trembles
as you dance in the oyster wash

and waves crack
like broken sidewalk around you

before day comes
and you resort to common life again

this morning when I opened my dream box,
all there was was the moon

Bart's Night Out

His need is to forget the small talk of love,
the whispered forevers that do not last,
the barbed-wire confessional of commitment
that always gets pushed against,
the endearments and promises,
things larger than either heart intended.

It's part of growing up, his twice-married father consoles,
as if words and straight shots assured some healing,
but even a schoolboy knows
that things really are darkest
just before they go completely black.

And the rest, there to remind
that people who can't bear to be alone
frequently are — the *papier-mâché* drunk at the rail,
tawdry waitresses, the spastic dancers who make him grin.
It is a registry of the ungainly and unloved,
those whose hides never proved tough enough,
who drink like fish wishing to be salmon,
to spawn once more before they spoil and die.

But we are all out of water, and the whiskey
is a long way from its source. Though
it distills our longing, it goes down hard,
topples us like slaughterhouse steers
until done and bewildered,
and no brighter than when we started,
we head back home nearly believing
it has been enough tonight
simply to beat first light back to the barn.

The Sex Researcher

It is all science to him:
the couples on campus arm and arm,
the wild ones tearing beneath the sheets,
old passions gone to seed at home.
He makes their numbers stand to account,
fixes ardor's level on the map,
but his measurement is always brief.

Yet this large picture omits himself,
idles like a transgression in a man
who has never experimented with an embrace.
Raw data is all he knows, not the girl
shaking grass tufts from her hair
or the monotonous waitress at the lake.

I suppose it beats cold fusion in a jar,
and none of us feels disarmed or cheated.
Though the cold stars go shooting into space,
sex's knowledge baffles, is continuously bold,
yet cannot for him be repeated.

Monet/Duet

"Would you two do one together?" he asked,
handing me the guitar. "We don't do duets," she said,
but, taking up the pick as if it were a brush,
I swirled her refusal until it became the debris of flowers.
Then a divine light overtook her, washed her in its calming hue,
and lavender settled like dusk on a river vista
until every waterway, beating like hearts in syncopation,
became a tribute to the scene. Its voice forsaken,
desire sought a cradle in the bluing waves,
and the eco-party emptied like Keats's village of its guests,
having already raised glasses of champagne in the mirror
in an act of self-regard that by its very nature canceled itself.

Then sensing it would be a shame to leave her this way,
I pictured the battles to be won upon her body
and daubed the gestures I have seen her leg make
a million times in carefree repetition. I painted the ways
she declines history, evades karma, the promise of her unyielding caress,
the way she saves her secrets for the end. She would saturate this canvas
with her tears — and I would lead her room to room in laughter
and bathe her where no wound was ever struck. I would tie us
together like two French centimes in a silk scarf.
I would doom her in my love and leave her lost,
but she would never invite me into one of her songs.

Calling in the Dark

this night a million crickets fiddle
what sways down under is love
and melodies of the dark,
then stillness while they gather breath

and flat and featureless rub
themselves without hope of light
or music enough to solve the riddle
that bows to unsatisfied desire

though every song is about death
even two notes may warm
a dream or burst into fire
and put things right

where they rise from the dirt
like nomad abos
troubadours crossing the hibiscus dateline
in shell necklaces and grass skirts

if only to meet this once
and strum each other like a chord
(then more than once)
and play away the night

The Sorrow of Lobsters

certain women look better wet
emerging from tired surf
or — imagine — the backseats
of taxis in the rain

in drought
you can see their mirages
glimmering in the far horizon

their names burble
on the lips of every lake
each well holds their promise

though we owe something to our dreams
there is much to be said for water
it shapes mountains
in the blowholes of whales
and sets silvery carp shivering
in their pools

in our own mouths
saliva logs our tongues
like butter

but in someone else's
French seems easy
the words made liquid
like warming snow

sometimes when I waken
in the night
sweating in this awkward carapace
of our love
I think of water

when I hold you to my ear
I always dream of home

Simple Division

this was once a field and a small forest
before the estates began to pile
and gave us something to see

now ashamed there are no trees
a woman packs a suitcase
because a new man offers roses

across a hundred households
this is the way families split
well, things that are are

and derive little benefit
from being explained
one looks for clarity

in simple promises
but every heart that opens
leaves a wound that never closes

... and Forty Nights

The storm that took us
wetted the way, drenching our bodies
as we melted like saltines
on an unsettled sea.

We clung like animals paired
in the hold, legs smeared
and sweaty, and the dull blear
of passion flooding our eyes.

Such passage was not easy,
our long month not enough,
so we rowed to land together
uneasy in the ark of our sadness,
until home at last and bone dry
I gave you back your skin.

Rheum and Coca-Cola

trusting in small things
you take the tablet
between thumb and finger
and lie back on your left side
afraid your heart might stop

every day your body
relaxes into itself
but unlearns its lesson
by nightfall

the bed is a nocturnal conscience
full of cats
always one awake
ready to warm himself
and monitor your steady breath

but outside noises
bring distance to mind
the barking dog finds you
when sleep can't

it is an old fear
you fumble again for the pills
another nightstand chaser
as you try to coil around yourself
in a patch of slumber

but aware in your drowse
and between sips
that something long ago
and much stronger than milk
has already been spilt

Washing the Cadavers

What is visible was once human:
a man who hosed vomit from the Twister
and hoisted a few with Ginsberg
before each found the answer to cancer.

The guy with the plastinated liver
guessed his way through an ESP test at Yale;
the donor to the brain bank
rode the rods to Georgia during the Depression.

The former waitress with the subluxated hip
and fibroid lungs reared nine children
while carting barbecue to cardiologists.
The macerated grandfather jumped ship

in Pusan harbor, drowned. Now you
lave their shoulders, cleanse grave wax
from spine and thorax; *livor mortis,*
the color of cornflowers, blooms

blue as a daughter's eyes. Your
butter-knife blade rasps the skin
of an executed felon dubbed Jethro
(to rhyme with Death Row)

by fresh osteopaths who have tied a bow
to his phenol-embalmed penis. Fervent
for your blush, they leave intra-abdominal notes,
envy your warming touch.

This one might have painted portraits
had his life not been left to the comics page;
his body, exposed, weeps a palette
the colors of a femoral nerve.

You note his scar, the moles, a tattoo,
the busted lip that longed to flatter
and all the curses one can imagine.

And because you are that one
and have looked at him, you can never
look at any of us the same way again.

The Student Research Conference

On the platform a young woman discourses
on tornadoes and droughts; then a blazered lad
in boots hammers on about corn fungus before the girl
in the session's last declares Hardy's Jude
a winsome dunce. They think these things are so;
their sources, unimpeachable, concur,
for they have examined zinc oxide in baby cream,
information visualization engines, rare earth,
sexism at Southfork. It is an unholy dream.

Their optimism is indigestible, like the diets
of non-native toads. It cannot be cured like a ham
or proclaimed away like dryads in the trees.
Their declarations are a kind of regression
into a past, still fuzzy, they did not live but still dream dull,
and the future, mended by Zantac, Viagra, and Paxil,
is the trinity of your middle age, not theirs.
The hereafter they see is full of outdoor recreation,
beneficial insects, on-line art, and mock industrial waste.

Call it youth's ambition to restate the world,
but what's coming is supernatural, soulless, all too,
a place unlikely to whisper much desire. That it won't say
just now doesn't matter; theirs is a world, neither new nor brave,
that science nor love will much want to save.

How To Make Love to the Same Woman Forever

die young

Simple Versions of Disaster

Despite the title *Simple Versions of Disaster*, Bradley's collection is simple neither in content nor in demands of poetic forms. ... He sees pain and disaster, whatever their scope, as precluding simple explanations. What remains then are the essential mysteries of human nature and the natural world. Bradley's poetry implies that artistic creation is redemptive for the artist, including the poet, and an inspiration for us all.

        Betsy Colquitt, *Texas Books in Review*

Simple Versions of Disaster contains poems that are about life's emotional explosions and the psychic craters they leave behind. ... Jerry Bradley's poems seem to give up their message readily to the reader, but then they keep ringing with the grace of their style and the ripples of their meanings. I think Bradley should be recognized as one of the charter members of the New Clarity School of Poetry.

        Richard Sale, University of North Texas Press

What is contained in this delightful collection of poetic observations is ... a remarkable wisdom that emerges from experiencing the disasters of everyday life.

        Clay Reynolds, *Fort Worth Star-Telegram*

Poet extraordinaire Jerry Bradley offers ... a volume of poetry that hits the eye with a fresh view of life that even a poetry hater can love. ... This book is a fine example of what purpose contemporary poetry must have, a relevancy to modern life.

        Texas Association of Creative Writing Newsletter

I like the wit, toughness, sensitivity, and complexity.

        Dick Heaberlin, *Western American Literature*

... an interesting range of formal strategies, from open-form stanzas to cinquains and sonnets.

        R. S. Gwynn, *Review of Texas Books*

How breathlessly this poet speaks. ... Lines of uncommon pungency jump out at the reader, forcing the reader to re-read their contexts. ... This is mighty fine writing.
  David Castleman, *Dusty Dog Reviews*

In a plethora of similes, the author tells us in free verse and scattered rhyme how each of life's experiences — birth, childhood, youth, sex, marriage, family, aging — comes to gloom. But Bradley, with his wit, craftsmanship, and irreverence makes the disasters interesting enough to entice the reader.
  Pauline D. Robertson, *Amarillo News-Globe*

Southwest settings provide the background for many of these powerful and haunting poems. Bradley relates the universal themes of love, life, and death to everyday topics: marriage, divorce, adolescence, geriatric promiscuity, crime, insomnia, and the despoliation of the land and its creatures.
  Books of the Southwest

About the Author

Jerry Bradley is Professor of English at Lamar University. He is the author of several books including *The Movement: British Poets of the 1950s* and his acclaimed first volume of poetry, *Simple Versions of Disaster*, which was commended by the *Dictionary of Literary Biography*. A member of the Texas Institute of Letters, he is past president of the Texas Association of Creative Writing Teachers. The current poetry editor of *Concho River Review*, Bradley was founder and editor for sixteen years of *New Mexico Humanities Review*. He has served as a member of the literature panel for the Texas Commission on the Arts and the New Mexico Arts Division and is past president of the Conference of College Teachers of English and the Southwest/Texas Popular Culture Association.

Among many awards Bradley has received during his distinguished career are the CCTE Frances Hernandez Teacher-Scholar of the Year (2005), the Texas College English Association Joe D. Thomas Scholar-Teacher of the Year (2000), the Boswell Poetry Prize (1996), and the CCTE British Literature Award (1996). He is a three-time Pushcart Prize nominee and was named Outstanding Alumnus of Midwestern State University College of Liberal Arts (2002).

Bradley's poetry has appeared in many literary magazines including the *New England Review*, *American Literary Review*, *Modern Poetry Studies*, *Poetry Magazine*, and *Southern Humanities Review*.

jerry.bradley@hotmail.com